A WORLD TREASURY
OF FOLK WISDOM

COMPILED AND EDITED BY

REYNOLD FELDMAN
AND CYNTHIA VOELKE

HarperSanFrancisco
A Division of HarperCollins*Publishers*

A WORLD TREASURY OF FOLK WISDOM. Copyright © 1992 by Reynold Feldman and Cynthia Voelke. All rights reserved. Printed in the United States of America. No part of this book may be used or reproduced in any manner whatsoever without written permission except in the case of brief quotations embodied in critical articles and reviews. For information address HarperCollins Publishers, 10 East 53rd Street, New York, NY 10022.

FIRST EDITION

Library of Congress Cataloging-in-Publication Data

A world treasury of folk wisdom / compiled by Reynold Feldman and Cynthia Voelke.
   ISBN 0–06–250319–7 (acid-free paper)
   1. Proverbs. I. Feldman, Reynold.   II. Voelke, Cynthia.
PN6405.W584   1992
398.9—dc20   91–58185
                                                         CIP

92 93 94 95 96 ❖ FAIR 1 2 3 4 5 6 7 8 9 10
This edition is printed on acid-free paper that meets the American National Standards Institute Z39.48 Standard.

To all my teachers, with love and gratitude
R. F.

To all those I have met on my path—the fools, the wise, and the loving—but especially to the new and innocent, Sam and Cody
C. V.

CONTENTS

ACKNOWLEDGMENTS

Never forget benefits done you,
regardless how small.
                    —Vietnamese proverb

Collecting proverbs for this book led us on a fascinating journey through time and place. From dusty used-bookstore shelves to modern research libraries, from conversations with relatives and friends of friends to telephone interviews with educators and diplomats, we sought our quarry everywhere. Proverbial sayings have existed in virtually every culture. Doubtless much has been lost, but much remains for those willing to search. We owe a debt of gratitude to an army of philologists, missionaries, anthropologists, and other collectors of folk wisdom, without whose work we would have been unable to create this book. Additional thanks go to the librarians who have carefully catalogued and preserved these works as well as guided us to them. Finally we wish to acknowledge the patience, help, and unfailing support of our friends, coworkers, and most especially our families. Special thanks go to two people: Roland Seboldt, our impresario and editor extraordinaire in the Twin Cities, and to Hilary Vartanian, our editorial guru and pathfinder in San Francisco.

We would also like to recognize the following institutions:

The St. Paul Public Library; the Minneapolis Public Library; the Wilson Library, University of Minnesota, Twin Cities; the Central American Resource Center, Minneapolis; the Minnesota State University System Office; the St. John's University Library, Collegeville, Minnesota; the Williams College Library; the A. C. Clark Library, Bemidji State University; the Northeastern Illinois University Library, Chicago; the Newberry Library, Chicago; the Northwestern University Library; the University Research Library, University of California Los Angeles; the Western Washington University Library; the Hamilton Graduate Library of the University of Hawaii, Manoa; and the Mansfield Library, University of Montana, Missoula.

Among the individuals who helped us in a variety of ways, large and small, we would like to cite the following:

Charles Graham and Nancy Pleiss, International Programs, Minnesota State University System; Samira Saleh; Aurelia Peterson; John Burton, Colleen Coghlan and Yolanda Dewar, Metropolitan State University; Garrett and Renata Thomson, University of Wisconsin, Oshkosh; Rod Henry, Bemidji State University; Loren Ekroth, University of Hawaii; Jim Green, Sisseton Wahpeton Community College; Charles Courtney, Society for Values in Higher Education; Dave Archambault, Standing Rock Community College; Sargon and Wilma Odishoo; Luis Serron, Normandale Community College; Roger Buffalo, American Indian Resource Center; Sally Hunter and Stana Mack, University of St. Thomas; Nina Mohr, Manhattan Beach

Public Library, Los Angeles County Library System; Anne Michelson, Australian Consulate-General, Chicago; Olav I. Torvik; Kim Calvillo, Nebraska Indian Community College; Juan Moreno, University of Minnesota; Ives Goddard, The Smithsonian; Maria de Landis, Embassy of Guatemala; and Marjorie Mack, Blackduck, Minnesota Public Library.

A Note to Our Readers: Our proverb collection, though large, is alive, well, and still growing. We would be happy to receive favorite proverbs or sayings that you did not find in the book. Please send them to the authors in care of:

The Scribes
7775 Glenda Court, Suite G1
Apple Valley, MN 55124

❧ INTRODUCTION

The French have a word for it. But then, so do the English, the
Spanish, and the Germans—not to mention the Jamaicans, the
Maoris, and the Zulus. Human beings in every culture have had to
deal with the identical questions of living and dying, of survival,
growth, relationship, and meaning. Fortunately our ancestors have
passed down their life learning in the form of short, easily remembered sayings. Variously called maxims, saws, apothegms, dicta, riddles, notions, analects, slogans, mottoes, epigrams, truisms, aphorisms, cliches, idioms, expressions, inscriptions, jingles, and refrains,
these pieces of anonymous wisdom are best known in English as
proverbs. This anthology is a treasury of proverbial wisdom from all
parts of the world.

Proverbs provide practical guidance for daily living. After all, "A
stitch in time saves nine." In fact many of the same truths in slightly
varied forms are widely found across cultures. The Welsh on their
rocky seacoast know that "those not ruled by the rudder will be ruled
by the rocks." Steer your life carefully or suffer the consequences. A
fisherfolk with a long history of seafaring, the Portuguese warn that
"the fish dies by its mouth." The temptation to speak out of turn, to
over-promise, or to give voice to anger has gotten each of us into
trouble more often than we care to remember. In a culture where silence is truly golden, the Japanese counsel that "if the bird hadn't
sung, it wouldn't have been shot." Calling attention to ourselves often

causes us problems. And the Iranians caution, "Trust in God but tie your camel." We should certainly have faith in the good all around us, but the same rain that waters our lawn will rust the lawn-mower left out in the yard.

We live in an increasingly global society. Technology brings us closer by the day. The wide world in its full history has hosted thousands of cultures and millions of souls. All these cultures and many individuals have contributed anonymously to the world's treasury of wisdom. This rich resource now forms a common heritage like the sea or the air that we can no longer ignore or take for granted. We live in a delicate, risk-filled time when we need every bit of wisdom to insure that we and our descendants will have a habitable planet and a rewarding life. On a personal level, a single bad choice can condemn us to a wasted life or a premature death. However, the wisdom of our collective ancestors is there for the taking. We can claim this birthright by learning and putting into practice what they have passed down to us.

There is a problem, however. Proverbs are very often inaccessible. They lie within the linguistic and cultural domains of other races and peoples. Usually we hear only those sayings common to our own culture or family. When we do encounter a proverb from another land, it is frequently in old-fashioned language or refers to people, places, or customs unfamiliar to us. In assembling this collection, we have combed old, out-of-print books, many written in the nineteenth century by British colonial officials. By choosing carefully and by updating the language, we have made the wit and wisdom of many of the world's peoples available to you.

This cross-cultural anthology is arranged in one hundred topical categories for easy use. The country or culture of origin is given after each proverb.

- Suspicious of a stranger with a get-rich-quick scheme? "When a thief kisses you, count your teeth." (Yiddish)

- Impatient for results? "Grain by grain, a loaf; stone by stone, a castle." (Yugoslavian)

- Three bad things happen to you back to back? "When fortune turns against you, even jelly breaks your teeth." (Iranian)

- Want to improve yourself? "Character is habit long continued." (Greek)

- Can't find your favorite novel? "A loan long continued usually confers ownership." (Irish)

- Wonder why you're reading this book? "All old sayings have something to them." (Icelandic)

This is a versatile book, with many possible applications. You may browse through these pages until you find an item that speaks to you, or you may take a more systematic approach. One possibility for the more analytical is to review, for one week, all the proverbs in a particular category. Then, focusing on that topic, see how you are

doing with it in your life. This approach resembles the famous self-de-
velopment program Benjamin Franklin described in his autobiogra-
phy. Franklin named thirteen virtues—temperance, silence, order,
resolution, frugality, industry, sincerity, justice, moderation, cleanli-
ness, tranquility, chastity, and humility. To make them into habits, he
paid special attention to one of them for a week. He then observed his
behavior. If the virtue in question was silence, he recorded the times
he spoke out of turn or talked too long when, in his later judgment,
he should have kept quiet. He then went on, in turn, to each virtue
and spent a week working on it. In this way he attempted to improve
his behavior and ultimately his character.

On a lighter note, you may swap favorite sayings with friends and
companions, or develop cross-cultural favors, like fortune cookies or
place cards, for a party. Or you may read the same proverb over and
over out loud with varying emphases and volume. You might try
recording such readings for yourself, then listening to them in a re-
laxed state. Practitioners of this meditative reading technique believe
that the essential meaning of the words will enter their conscious-
ness in a deeper way and influence their behavior more profoundly
than silent reading.

Writers, whether professionals, amateurs, or students, will dis-
cover resources to underscore a point or dissolve writer's block.
Editors of newsletters will find dozens of apt sayings to spice up an ar-
ticle or fill out an empty space on a page. Public speakers may hit
upon just the right note with which to begin or end a speech. This an-

thology may also help those who are learning English to acquire vocabulary and increase reading skills while becoming acquainted with wisdom from many lands. As the workplace the world over becomes culturally more diverse, these collected sayings can be useful in helping employees better understand their fellow workers. No doubt there are other uses for this book that we hope readers will share with us, for we believe its possibilities are almost endless.

Finally wisdom is about trying to make wise choices and doing the right thing. "Proverbs," the people of Sierra Leone say, "are the daughters of experience." Since one can cultivate the habit of learning from others, then, "A word to the wise," per the Latin maxim, "may be sufficient." The Russians instruct us that "there is no proverb without a grain of truth." Whatever your reason for reading this book, we hope, first, that you will be entertained, and second, that those grains will grow strongly within you and will enrich your life. Enjoy!

Reynold Feldman and Cynthia Voelke
Saint Paul, Minnesota

A World Treasury of Folk Wisdom

ADVERSITY

When you fall into a pit, you either die or get out.

Chinese

Each cross has its own inscription.

English

A stumble is not a fall.

Haitian

People in trouble remember Allah.

Hausa (West African)

Difficulties make you a jewel.

Japanese

Every tear has a smile behind it.

Iranian

What cannot be cured must be endured.

Scottish

Spare us what we can learn to endure.

Yiddish

Give advice; if people don't listen, let adversity teach them.

Ethiopian

No pain, no gain.

American

 ## ADVICE

A good example is the best sermon.

English

Good advice is often annoying—bad advice never is.

French

In night there is counsel.

Greek

Who are the deafest? Those who won't listen to good advice.

Sanskrit

Teeth placed before the tongue give good advice.

Italian

Don't give cherries to pigs or advice to fools.

Irish

Advice after mischief is like medicine after death.

Danish

It is easy to advise the wise.

Serbian

Seek advice but use your own common sense.

Yiddish

Advise no one to go to war or marry.

Spanish

〰 AMBITION

There's no eel so small but it hopes to become a whale.

German

Ambition destroys its possessor.

Hebrew

If you must be a servant, serve the rich; if you must be a dog, be a temple dog.

Laotian

The person who asks for little deserves nothing.

Mexican

Ambition begets vexations.

Singhalese

Aim high in your career but stay humble in your heart.

Korean

People seek out big-shots as flies seek out the elephant's tail.

Indonesian

If you would get ahead, be a bridge.

Welsh

You jump, but you come down all the same.

Martinican

Go for it!

American

 ## ANGER

The anger of the prudent never shows.

Burmese

Anger is often more hurtful than the injury that caused it.

English

Anger has no eyes.

Malay

A hand ready to hit may cause you great trouble.

Maori

Postpone today's anger until tomorrow.

Tagalog (Filipino)

The hot sun melts the snows; when anger comes, wisdom goes.

Hindi (Asian Indian)

If you kick a stone in anger, you'll hurt your own foot.

Korean

A word spoken in anger may mar an entire life.

Greek

Anger is a short madness.

Dutch

There's nothing worse than a person looking for a quarrel.

Serbian

✍ Appearance and Reality

Two things cannot be hidden: being astride a camel and being pregnant.

Lebanese

The teeth that laugh are also those that bite.

Hausa (West African)

Anything with scales counts as a fish.

Malay

A person who is always nice is not always nice.

Polish

What is true by lamplight is not always true by sunlight.

French

The price of your hat isn't the measure of your brain.

African-American

Though a cage may be made of gold, it is still a cage.

Mexican

One who pretends reluctance is like a turtle being taken
to water.

Lakota (Native American)

Froth is not beer.

Dutch

An illiterate king is a crowned ass.

English

 ## APPROPRIATENESS

When the music changes, so does the dance.

Hausa (West African)

What good is giving sugar to the dead?

Kashmiri

Don't use an ax to embroider.

Malay

When they gave the donkey flowers to smell, it ate them.

Armenian

Sun is good for cucumbers, rain for rice.

Vietnamese

If you enter a goat stable, bleat; if you enter a water buffalo stable, bellow.

Indonesian

Hold short services for minor gods.

Nepalese

Carve the peg by looking at the hole.

Korean

Don't plant a seed in the sea.

Swahili (East African)

The point of the needle must pass first.

Ethiopian

ART AND CREATIVITY

An artist lives everywhere.

English

Poetry moves heaven and earth.

Japanese

The block of wood should not dictate to the carver.

Maori

Even the best song becomes tiresome if heard too often.

Korean

People who do not break things first will never learn to create anything.

Tagalog (Filipino)

Every art requires the whole person.

French

A thousand artisans, a thousand plans.

Chinese

If you fail to practice your art, it will soon disappear.

German

A picture is a poem without words.

Latin

A good spectator also creates.

Swiss

ATTITUDE

When what you want doesn't happen, learn to want what does.

Arabic

A clever person turns great troubles into little ones and little ones into none at all.

Chinese

All happiness is in the mind.

English

To be willing is to be able.

French

Nothing is easy to the unwilling.

Gaelic

If it were not for hope, the heart would break.

Greek

The heart at rest sees a feast in everything.

Hindi (Asian Indian)

The dog that wags its tail won't be beaten.

Japanese

The person who truly desires to die will not complain if buried standing up.

Mexican

With a stout heart, a mouse can lift an elephant.

Tibetan

AUTHENTICITY

The shadow should be the same length as the body.
Indonesian

Cutting off a mule's ears doesn't make it a horse.
Creole

You can't get rice by pounding bran.
Burmese

A wild goose never laid a tame egg.
Gaelic

Cows have no business in horseplay.
Jamaican

Be not water, taking the tint of all colors.
Syrian

Fishing without a net is merely bathing.
Hausa (West African)

When a mother calls her child "bastard," you can take her word for it.

Yiddish

A boor remains a boor even if sleeping on silken pillows.

Danish

Don't take any wooden nickels!

American

BALANCE AND MODERATION

Don't hang your hat higher than you can reach.

Belizean

One can never have too much of a good thing.

American

Hands that give also receive.

Ecuadoran

Too much breaks the bag.

Spanish

If God wants people to suffer, he sends them too much understanding.

Yiddish

Strong attachment is difficult—it makes one mad or kills.

Moroccan

Where there is sunshine, there is also shade.

Kashmiri

Even in Mecca people make money.

Hausa (West African)

Going beyond is as bad as falling short.

Chinese

God did not create hurry.

Finnish

 ## Basic Truths

Shrouds are made without pockets.

Yiddish

You can't see the whole sky through a bamboo tube.

Japanese

Agreements should be clearly expressed, and chocolate should be served thick.

Mexican

Wherever you go, you can't get rid of yourself.

Polish

A crown is no cure for a headache.

English

All the treasures of the earth can't bring back one lost moment.

French

The baby who doesn't cry isn't nursed.

Latin American

Memory is life's clock.

Spanish

Where is there a tree not shaken by the wind?

Armenian

The afternoon knows what the morning never suspected.

Swedish

⬛ BEAUTY

If you are ugly, be winsome.

Tunisian

One cannot make soup out of beauty.

Estonian

Beauty is a good letter of introduction.

German

Even the fall of a dancer is a somersault.

Singhalese

Butterflies come to pretty flowers.

Korean

Beauty without virtue is a flower without perfume.

French

Desire beautifies even what is ugly.

Spanish

A beautiful thing is never perfect.

Egyptian

The face of water is beautiful, but it is not good to sleep on.

Ashanti (West African)

Handsome is as handsome does.

English

Books and Writers

Even the best writer has to erase.

Spanish

If you believe everything you read, better not read.

Japanese

There is no worse robber than a bad book.

Italian

A goose quill is more dangerous than a lion's claw.

English

Every age has its book.

Arabic

The sight of books removes sorrows from the heart.

Moroccan

A library is a repository of medicine for the mind.

Greek

The walking-stick reaches many lands, the word many more.

Finnish

A good book praises itself.

German

Beware the person of one book.

Latin

 ## Business

The gods sell all things to hard labor.

Greek

If you would be rich in a year, you may be hanged in six months.

Italian

If you give orders and leave, the work won't get done.

Portuguese

When the tiger kills, the jackal profits.

Afghan

A person without a smiling face should not open a shop.

Chinese

A work ill done must be twice done.

Welsh

If you have nothing to lose, you can try everything.

Yiddish

Creditors have better memories than debtors.

English

Be quick to follow up an advantage.

Maori

If you bathe, get thoroughly wet.

Malay

BUYING AND SELLING

They are most cheated who cheat themselves.

Danish

Little is spent with difficulty, much with ease.

Thai

Do not expect speed from a cheap horse—it will only neigh.

Hausa (West African)

Buying on credit is robbing next year's crop.

African-American

Better to sell with regret than to keep with regret.

Swiss

Making money selling manure is better than losing money selling musk.

Egyptian

Venture a small fish to catch a great one.

English

The spider and the fly can't make a bargain.

Jamaican

If you buy things you don't need, you'll soon be selling things you do.

Pampango (Filipino)

Don't buy someone else's problems.

Chinese

 ## CAUTION AND CARE

Measure a thousand times, cut once.

Turkish

The crab that walks too far falls into the pot.

Haitian

If you call one wolf, you invite the pack.

Bulgarian

Sleeping people can't fall down.

Japanese

Fish don't get caught in deep water.

Malay

Though honey is sweet, don't lick it off a briar.

Irish

Because we focused on the snake, we missed the scorpion.

Egyptian

Never reveal the bottom of your purse or the depth of your mind.

Italian

Beware a rickety wall, a savage dog, and a quarrelsome person.

Iranian

Whoever has a tail of straw should not get close to the fire.

Latin American

CHARACTER AND VIRTUE

Character is habit long continued.

Greek

The eagle does not catch flies.

Latin

Virtue is not knowing but doing.

Japanese

Where you were born is less important than how you live.

Turkish

People show their character by what they laugh at.

German

That which is a sin in others is a virtue in ourselves.

Chilean

You can't stop a pig from wallowing in the mud.

Yoruba (West African)

Character is easier kept than recovered.

English

If you make yourself into a doormat, people will wipe their feet on you.

Belizean

If you are not good for yourself, how can you be good for others?

Spanish

COMMON SENSE

It's a foolish sheep that makes the wolf its confessor.

Italian

Don't do all you can, spend all you have, believe all you hear, or tell all you know.

English

Even a fish wouldn't get into trouble if it kept its mouth shut.

Korean

Don't jump high in a low-ceilinged room.

Czech

Common sense is not so common.

French

Medicine left in the container can't help.

Yoruba (West African)

It takes a heap of licks to strike a nail in the dark.

African-American

It is better to prevent than to cure.

Peruvian

If you can't bite, better not show your teeth.

Yiddish

If you are hiding, don't light a fire.

Ghanaian

COMPARABLE WORTH

That which is mine makes other people's things seem strange.

Sumerian

Better a diamond with a flaw than a pebble without.

Chinese

It is better to suffer for truth than to prosper by falsehood.

Danish

Better is better.

German

If you think your bundle of dirty clothes too heavy, try picking up your neighbor's.

Virgin Islander

Being happy is better than being king.

Hausa (West African)

Better a good hope than a bad possession.

Spanish

If you turn into a dog, be sure to choose a rich family.

Japanese

A clock that stands still is better than one that goes wrong.

Yiddish

It's better to sleep on the floor in an incense shop than in a bed in a fishmarket.

Vietnamese

CONDUCT OF LIFE

Do good and then do it again.

Welsh

One should speak little with others and much with oneself.

Danish

Honor is better than honors.

Flemish

One should learn to sail in all winds.

Italian

Do not allow sins to get beyond creeping.

Hawaiian

A day is lost if one has not laughed.

French

Hurry is good only for catching flies.

Russian

As long as you live, keep learning how to live.

Latin

Promise little and do much.

Hebrew

It is better to return a borrowed pot with a little something you last cooked in it.

Omaha (Native American)

 ## CONSCIENCE

A clear conscience is more valuable than wealth.

Tagalog (Filipino)

No sin is hidden to the soul.

Bengali (Asian Indian)

Conscience cannot be compelled.

English

The horse may run quickly, but it can't escape its own tail.

Russian

A clear conscience shines not only in the eyes.

Lebanese

Old sin makes new shame.

English

Conscience is as good as a thousand witnesses.

Italian

A good conscience is better than a big wage.

Jamaican

To ask is a temporary shame; not to ask, an eternal one.

Japanese

A virtuous person sleeps well.

Thai

 ## CONTENTMENT

The greatest tranquility is when we desire nothing.

Middle Eastern

A harvest of peace grows from seeds of contentment.

Kashmiri

If they had cereal, they'd want gumbo.

Haitian

Blessed are those who can please themselves.

Zulu (South African)

When you can't find peace within yourself, it's useless to seek it elsewhere.

French

Jupiter himself cannot please everyone.

Latin

The person who lives in a quiet house has plenty.

Maori

Where the heart is, there is happiness.

Iranian

The contented person can never be ruined.

Chinese

The truly rich are those who enjoy what they have.

Yiddish

 ## COURAGE AND FEAR

If you are afraid of something, you give it power over you.

Moroccan

Heroism consists of hanging on one minute longer.

Norwegian

Worry often gives a small thing a big shadow.

Swedish

The brave person regards dying as going home.

Chinese

If you fear God, you won't fear humans.

Albanian

Our fears always outnumber our dangers.

Latin

One with the courage to laugh is master of the world almost as much as the person ready to die.

Italian

Fear the person who fears you.

Middle Eastern

There's no medicine for fear.

Scottish

The blind person is not afraid of ghosts.

Burmese

✎ COURTESY AND RESPECT

No strength within, no respect without.

Kashmiri

Many meet the gods, but few salute them.

Latin

If you owe a dog anything, call him "sir."

East Asian

Excellent people are honored wherever they go.

Tibetan

Never spend time with people who don't respect you.

Maori

When you go to a donkey's house, don't talk about ears.

Jamaican

Kind words conquer.

Tamil (Asian Indian)

Nice words are free, so choose ones that please another's ears.

Vietnamese

Too much politeness conceals deceit.

Chinese

To speak·ill of anyone is to speak ill of yourself.

Afghan

 ## CRITICISM

The bad plowman quarrels with his ox.

Korean

The human tongue is more poisonous than a bee's sting.

Vietnamese

Worthless people blame their karma.

Burmese

Don't call the alligator big-mouth till you have crossed the river.

Belizean

Accusing the times is but excusing ourselves.

English

Cussing the weather is mighty poor farming.

African-American

The rattan basket criticizes the palm-leafed bag, yet both are full of holes.

Filipino

The breath of others always stinks.

Lithuanian

Those who can't dance say the music is no good.

Jamaican

It is easier to criticize than to do better.

Swiss

CYNICISM

The good dog never gets a good bone.

Martinican

There is never trust without loss.

Basque

Remember to distrust.

Greek

There are a thousand roads to every wrong.

Polish

The hero appears only when the tiger is dead.

Burmese

Don't be so clever; cleverer ones than you are in jail.

Russian

Few are fit to be entrusted with themselves.

English

You go out for wool but come back shorn.

Peruvian

Good guys finish last.

American

The good white man dies, the bad one remains.

Haitian

DEATH AND DYING

Death is a black camel that kneels at everyone's gate.

Turkish

The white flower has bloomed—it is time to go to sleep outside.

Fijian

Death does not take the old but the ripe.

Russian

The bucket goes down in the well every day—some day it won't come up.

Virgin Islander

Six feet of earth make us all equal.

Italian

There is no dying by proxy.

French

Dying while young is a boon in old age.

Yiddish

A person has learned much who has learned how to die.

German

Death keeps no calendar.

English

People live like birds in a wood: When the time comes, each takes flight.

Chinese

 DESTINY

The fated thing will happen.

Gaelic

Individuals must stand high who would see their own destiny.

Danish

Tie your camel, then trust in Allah.

Arabic

If you're fated to drown, you may die in a teaspoon of water.

Yiddish

Karma is the mother and karma the father.

Burmese

A person born to be a flower pot will not go beyond the porch.

Mexican

You can't flee your lot nor share it with another.

Afghan

As individuals go their own way, destiny accompanies them.

Tamil (Asian Indian)

You often meet your destiny on the road you take to avoid it.

French

Even the stone you trip on is part of your fate.

Japanese

Differences

Even a sheet of paper has two sides.

Japanese

The lion believes that everyone shares its state of mind.

Mexican

People live with their own idiosyncrasies and die of their own illnesses.

Vietnamese

Every head is a world.

Cuban

Different sores have different salves.

English

Every burro has its own saddle.

Ecuadoran

Different fields, different grasshoppers; different seas, different fish.

Indonesian

Even children of the same mother look different.

Korean

Each bay, its own wind.

Fijian

One person can burn water, while another can't even burn oil.

Kashmiri

⬛ DISCRETION

Having two ears and one tongue, we should listen twice as much as we speak.

Turkish

Discretion in speech is more important than eloquence.

English

Stones decay; words last.

Samoan

All food is fit to eat, but not all words are fit to speak.

Haitian

Words should be weighed, not counted.

Yiddish

Silence is sometimes the answer.

Estonian

When the mouth stumbles, it is worse than the foot.

Oji (West African)

Forethought is easy, repentance hard.

Chinese

There is nothing that can't be made worse by telling.

Latin

The tongue has no bones, yet it breaks bones.

Greek

 EDUCATION

Doubt is the key to knowledge.

Iranian

One who is afraid of asking is ashamed of learning.

Danish

Instruction in youth is like engraving in stone.

Moroccan

Learning makes people fit company for themselves.

English

Necessity is a great teacher.

Mexican

Without learning, without eyes.

Lithuanian

The one who teaches is the giver of eyes.

Tamil (Asian Indian)

With time even a bear can learn to dance.

Yiddish

Not to know is bad, not to want to know is worse.

Gambian

Even a thief takes ten years to learn his trade.

Japanese

ELOQUENCE

When the heart is full the tongue will speak.

Scottish

A person who talks a lot is sometimes right.

Spanish

If a person's mouth were silent, another part would speak.

Arabic

The inarticulate speak longest.

Japanese

Often there is eloquence in a silent look.

Latin

There is nothing so eloquent as a rattlesnake's tail.

Apache (Native American)

Even a soft speech has its own poison.

Syrian

A gentle word opens an iron gate.

Bulgarian

The mouth is not sweetened by saying, "Honey, honey."

Turkish

Better one living word than a hundred dead ones.

German

 ## EXPERIENCE

By crawling, a child learns to stand.

Hausa (West African)

An old ox makes a straight furrow.

Spanish

A stumble may prevent a fall.

English

If you are not a fish, how can you tell if the fish are happy?

Chinese

The tongue of experience has the most truth.

Arabic

Necessity teaches all things.

German

Only the sufferers know how their bellies ache.

Burmese

You learn through mistakes—no one was born a master.

Swiss

The person with burnt fingers asks for tongs.

Samoan

By committing foolish acts, one learns wisdom.

Singhalese

 **FAITH**

What one hopes for is always better than what one has.

Ethiopian

Faith is confirmed by the heart, confessed by the tongue, and acted upon by the body.

Sufi

To believe with certainty, we must begin by doubting.

Polish

The god who made the mouth will provide the food.

Nepalese

Blessed is the moon; it goes but it comes back again.

Samoan

Have faith—God calls forth life even from eggs.

Kashmiri

Faith keeps the world going.

Hindi (Asian Indian)

When God gives a child, he also gives the clothing.

Estonian

The God who gave us teeth will also give us bread.

Czech

The strength of the heart comes from the soundness of
the faith.

Arabic

 FAME

Tigers die and leave their skins; people die and leave their names.

Japanese

Our shadow will follow us.

Tamil (Asian Indian)

If you hold high office, the whole village will share your fame.

Vietnamese

Falling is easier than rising.

Irish

Put a rope around your neck and many will be happy to drag you along.

Egyptian

There's no glory without sacrifice.

Bicol (Filipino)

Become famous, then go to sleep.

Latin American

A puff of wind and popular praise weigh alike.

English

When the leopard is large, it will be seen by everybody.

Yoruba (West African)

A good name is a second inheritance.

German

FLATTERY AND PRAISE

A flatterer has water in one hand and fire in the other.

German

Flattery is sweet food for those who can swallow it.

Danish

Too much praise is really mockery.

Ilocano (Filipino)

One who speaks fair words feeds you with an empty spoon.

Italian

A flatterer is a secret enemy.

Hungarian

Chickens don't praise their own soup.

Martinican

Fair words can buy a horse on credit

Trinidadian

Every peddler praises his own needles.

Portuguese

If you would be praised, die.

Welsh

Self-praise is no recommendation.

Romanian

Food and Hunger

No clock is more regular than the belly.

French

Suppers have killed more than doctors have ever cured.

Spanish

Let your head be more than a funnel to your stomach.

German

Epicures dig their graves with their teeth.

Tamil (Asian Indian)

Even food can attack.

Maori

Those who are one in food are one in life.

Malagasy

What good is honor when you're starving?

Yiddish

The full person does not understand the needs of the hungry.

Irish

Plenty sits still, hunger is a wanderer.

Zulu (South African)

The hungry fowl wakes early.

Jamaican

FOOLISHNESS

Fools are like other folks as long as they are silent.

Danish

If you follow a fool, you're a fool yourself.

Jamaican

Fools and scissors require good handling.

Japanese

It's the fool's sheep that break loose twice.

Ashanti (West African)

Only the foolish visit the land of the cannibals.

Maori

The half-wit spoke, and the brainless believed.

Iranian

The complete fool is half prophet.

Yiddish

The fool is thirsty in the midst of water.

Ethiopian

The fool never undertakes little.

Czech

A fool's soul is always dancing on the tip of his tongue.

Arabic

FORTUNE

One often gets what one disdains.

Vietnamese

Every cloud has a silver lining.

American

When fortune calls, offer her a chair.

Yiddish

Change yourself, and fortune will change.

Portuguese

Don't trust in fortune until you are in heaven.

Tagalog (Filipino)

Good luck comes in slender currents, misfortune in a rolling tide.

Irish

Fortune favors the bold.

Latin

Fortune and misfortune are two buckets in the same well.

German

Even the devil slaves for the fortunate.

Nepalese

People are the architects of their own fortune.

Spanish

FREEDOM AND SLAVERY

Chains of gold are stronger than chains of iron.

English

A slave has no choice.

Kenyan

The person who has been a slave from birth does not value rebellion.

Yoruba (West African)

A country without freedom is like a prisoner with shackled hands.

Ilocano (Filipino)

Like a fish, one should look for a hole in the net.

Samoan

To receive a favor is to sell one's liberty.

Japanese

The tyrant is only the slave turned inside out.

Egyptian

They are not free who drag their chains after them.

French

A person is still a slave whose limbs alone are free.

German

Liberty has no price.

Spanish

FRIENDS AND FOES

Avoid a friend who covers you with his wings and destroys you with his beak.

Spanish

One enemy is too many; one hundred friends are too few.

Icelandic

Who is mighty? One who makes an enemy into a friend.

Hebrew

Tell me your friends, and I'll tell you who you are.

Assyrian

You never really know your friends from your enemies until the ice breaks.

Eskimo

Though your enemy is the size of an ant, regard him as an elephant.

Danish

The wolf and the dog agree at the expense of the goat—
which together they eat.

Basque

Better a thousand enemies outside the tent than one within.

Arabic

Cold tea and cold rice are bearable, but not cold looks and
cold words.

Japanese

An intelligent enemy is better than a stupid friend.

Senegalese

FRIENDSHIP

A friend—one soul, two bodies.

Chinese

Don't let grass grow on the path of friendship.

Blackfoot (Native American)

One leg cannot dance alone.

East African

A new broom sweeps clean, but an old broom knows the corners.

Virgin Islander

Life without a friend is death without a witness.

Spanish

A friend's eye is a good mirror.

Gaelic

When I eat your bread, I sing your song.

German

Better one true friend than a hundred relatives.

Italian

Make a friend when you don't need one.

Jamaican

A stone from the hand of a friend is an apple.

Moroccan

 GENEROSITY

Good people, like clouds, receive only to give away.

Asian Indian

If you have, give; if you lack, seek.

Malay

What you do to others will bear fruit in you.

Singhalese

You may light another's candle at your own without loss.

Danish

The charitable give out at the door, while God puts in at the window.

English

Give good and get good.

Estonian

Give even an onion graciously.

Afghan

A thing is bigger for being shared.

Gaelic

Poor people entertain with the heart.

Haitian

The best generosity is that which is quick.

Arabic

 GOD

Even God cannot make two mountains without a valley in between.

Gaelic

God is a good worker but loves to be helped.

Basque

For a weaving begun, God sends threads.

Italian

God gives to us according to the measure of our hearts.

Iranian

There are four things Allah cannot do: lie, deny himself, die, or look favorably on sin.

Arabic

Search yourself, and you will find Allah.

Kurdish

God created a world full of little worlds.

Yiddish

Solitude is full of God.

Serbian

God often visits us, but most of the time we are not at home.

French

Every day is a messenger of God.

Russian

 ## Good and Evil

The existence of the sea means the existence of pirates.

Malay

No one is hurt by doing the right thing.

Hawaiian

Public money is like holy water: people help themselves.

Italian

Weeds never perish.

Flemish

There is no escape from the net of heaven.

Japanese

Do good and forget it; do ill and remember it.

Maltese

People aren't good unless others are made better by them.

Welsh

Do good and care not to whom.

Portuguese

A good tree can lodge ten thousand birds.

Burmese

The pleasure of doing good is the only one that will not wear out.

Chinese

 ## GOSSIP

Not everything you hear is good for talk.

Jamaican

Four horses cannot overtake the tongue.

Chinese

Words have no wings but they can fly a thousand miles.

Korean

Sin is carried in the mouth.

Samoan

Loose lips sink ships.

American

A word and a stone let go cannot be recalled.

Spanish

It is easier to dam a river than stop gossip.

Moro (Filipino)

You can't sew buttons on your neighbor's mouth.

Russian

Gossips always suspect that others are talking about them.

Yoruba (West African)

You can lock your door from a thief, but not from a damn liar.

Virgin Islander

GRATITUDE

When you drink water, remember the mountain spring.

Chinese

When the heat is past, you forget about shade trees.

Japanese

There is nothing like deprivation to excite gratitude for small mercies.

Spanish

When eating a fruit, think of the person who planted the tree.

Vietnamese

If something that was going to chop off our head only knocked off our cap, we should be grateful.

Yoruba (West African)

Thanks cost nothing.

Creole

In a small house God has his corner, in a big house he has to stand in the hall.

Swedish

The one being carried does not realize how far away the town is.

Nigerian

The giver should forget, but the receiver should remember forever.

Polish

Even the hen looks toward heaven when she drinks.

Albanian

 GREED

Unjustly got wealth is snow sprinkled with hot water.

Chinese

Ants die in sugar.

Malay

Trying to get everything, you often get nothing.

Ivatan (Filipino)

The covetous person is always in want.

Irish

A greedy person and a pauper are practically one and
the same.

Swiss

To ask a favor from a miser is like trying to make a hole in the water.

Armenian

A miser is like a person with bread who is starving.

Middle Eastern

A greedy father has thieves for children.

Serbian

The poor lack much, but the greedy more.

Swiss

A miser's money takes the place of wisdom.

Dutch

 ## HABIT

Live with vultures, become a vulture; live with crows, become a crow.

Laotian

It is hard for an ex-king to become a night watchman.

Kashmiri

A pig used to dirt turns its nose up at rice.

Japanese

Strange smoke irritates the eyes.

Lithuanian

Everything is formed by habit, even praying.

Egyptian

Break the legs of an evil custom.

Italian

Nothing is difficult if you're used to it.

Indonesian

Wherever you go, habit follows.

Ilocano (Filipino)

What is learned in the cradle lasts to the grave.

French

An old error has more friends than a new truth.

Danish

HEALTH AND WELLNESS

Better ten times ill than one time dead.

Yiddish

If you would live long, open your heart.

Bulgarian

Sickness comes on horseback but leaves on foot.

Walloon

Before supper walk a little; after supper do the same.

Latin

When the heart is at ease, the body is healthy.

Chinese

God heals, but the doctor gets the money.

Flemish

Before healing others, heal yourself.

Gambian

The pain is sometimes preferable to the treatment.

Behari (Asian Indian)

A good life prevents wrinkles.

Spanish

One day in perfect health is much.

Arabic

HEAVEN AND HELL

Hell is wherever heaven is not.

English

Pleasures are transient—honors immortal.

Greek

You don't have to die: heaven and hell are in this world too.

Japanese

There are no fans in hell.

East Asian

Earth is but a marketplace; heaven is home.

Yoruba (West African)

Hell shared with a sage is better than paradise with a fool.

Yiddish

In heaven you won't hear the mosquitoes.

Finnish

Continue to do good, and heaven will come down to you.

Hawaiian

Hell is full of ingrates.

Spanish

When the devil leaves, heaven comes in.

Cree (Native American)

HOME AND FAMILY

A lonely person is at home everywhere.

Russian

Brothers and sisters are as close as hands and feet.

Vietnamese

Every worm has its hole.

Yiddish

A hearth of your own is worth gold.

Danish

A house full of people is a house full of different points of view.

Maori

Mules make a great fuss about their ancestors having been asses.

German

The sun at home warms better than the sun outside.

Albanian

To forget one's ancestors is to be a brook without a source, a tree without a root.

Chinese

Come see me and come live with me are two different things.

Virgin Islander

A guest sticks a nail in the wall even if he stays only one night.

Polish

THE HUMAN COMEDY

The person sins, then blames Satan for it.

Afghan

Make a meal, and contention will cease.

Hebrew

Nothing dries sooner than tears.

Italian

Sugarcane is always sweet—people only sometimes.

Burmese

The stargazer's toe is often stubbed.

Russian

One ass calls the other a pack animal.

Yiddish

The sparrow flying behind the hawk thinks the hawk is fleeing.

Japanese

Even Buddhist priests of the same temple quarrel occasionally.

Singhalese

Generally we love ourselves more than we hate others.

English

What is much desired is not believed when it comes.

Spanish

 ## HYPOCRISY

Everyone is friendly if you have money; otherwise there are only strangers.

Nepalese

The mouth prays to Buddha, but the heart is full of evil.

Vietnamese

All are not saints who go to church.

Italian

What the mulla says, you must do; what he does, you must not do.

Kashmiri

Hypocrites kick with their hind feet while licking with their tongues.

Russian

They call her aunt only when her cucumbers are ripe.

Burmese

Beware of the person with two faces.

Dutch

If you would rise in the world, veil ambition with the forms of humanity.

Chinese

You can't carry two faces under one hat.

Jamaican

Outside a sheep, inside a wolf.

Greek

 IDLENESS

Sleepy turtles never catch up with the sunrise.

Jamaican

Work and you will be strong; sit and you will stink.

Moroccan

A big blanket makes a person sleep late.

Bahamian

Lazy people are always eager to be doing something.

French

Put off for one day and ten days will pass.

Korean

Idleness is to be dead at the limbs but alive within.

Fijian

The lazy sweat when they eat and complain of the cold when they work.

Finnish

Offer the lazy an egg, and they'll want you to peel it for them.

Lithuanian

It is easier to believe than to go and ask.

Serbian

The lazy person must work twice.

Latin American

 **IMPOSSIBILITY**

One sesame seed won't make oil.

Burmese

Fish are not caught by a birdcall.

English

You can't straighten a snake by placing it in a bamboo tube.

Japanese

No river can return to its source, yet all rivers must have a beginning.

Native American

To believe a thing impossible is to make it so.

French

A kitchen knife cannot carve its own handle.

Korean

You cannot shave a man's head in his absence.
Yoruba (West African)

You can wash your body but not your soul.
Yiddish

A thousand people cannot undress a naked person.
Greek

It is impossible to bend the arm of God.
Maasai (East African)

 ## INDEBTEDNESS

Don't worry if you borrow—worry if you lend.
Russian

Never promise a poor person, and never owe a rich one.
Brazilian

A loan, though old, is not a gift.

Hungarian

Sins and debts are always more than we think them to be.

English

If you want to know the value of money, go and borrow some.

Spanish

Nothing seems expensive on credit.

Czech

Interest on debts grows without rain.

Yiddish

A debt is always new.

Estonian

A loan long continued usually confers ownership.

Irish

An old debt is better than an old grudge.

Jamaican

JEALOUSY AND ENVY

Jealousy is a pain that seeks what caused it.

German

It is better to be envied than pitied.

Greek

Envious persons never compliment, they only swallow.

Mexican

Envy shoots at others and wounds itself.

English

Great trees are envied by the wind.

Japanese

Envy has no rest.
Middle Eastern

When the rain falls in the valley, the hill gets angry.
Yoruba (West African)

The moon does not trouble itself about the howling of dogs.
Italian

Compete—don't envy.
Yemeni

On seeing a horse, a walker wants to ride.
Korean

Journeys

If you are going a long way, go slowly.
Ilocano (Filipino)

The more you ask how much longer it will take, the longer the journey seems.

Maori

A turtle travels only when it sticks its neck out.

Korean

Don't boast when you set out, but when you get there.

Russian

When you go, the road is rough; when you return, smooth.

Thai

Don't bypass a town where there's a friend.

Malagasy

A day of traveling will bring a basketful of learning.

Vietnamese

Little by little one walks far.

Peruvian

When you have no companion, look to your walking-stick.

Albanian

The world is the traveler's inn.

Afghan

 ## JOY AND SORROW

Sorrow doesn't kill, but it blights.

Russian

A bend in the human heart cannot be seen.

Maori

The person who loves sorrow will always find something to mourn about.

Danish

The person who gets stuck on petty happiness will not attain great happiness.

Tibetan

Sorrow doesn't kill—reckless joy does.
Yoruba (West African)

Sorrow is to the soul what the worm is to wood.
Turkish

The bridge between joy and sorrow is not long.
German

If it weren't for sorrow and bad times, every day would be Christmas.
Lithuanian

One does not live on joy or die of sorrow.
Yiddish

The end of mirth is the beginning of sorrow.
Dutch

 JUSTICE

Losers are always in the wrong.

Spanish

It is cruelty to the innocent not to punish the guilty.

Syrian

God lets things go—but only to a point.

Swiss

God's mill goes slowly but grinds fine.

German

They are cheated most who cheat themselves.

Danish

A good cat deserves a good rat.

French

Curses are like chickens; they come home to roost.

Greek

The deceitful have no friends.

Hindi (Asian Indian)

Today my turn, tomorrow yours.

Samoan

Laws catch flies, but let hornets go free.

Scottish

KNOWLEDGE AND IGNORANCE

What the dawn will bring is not known.

Ethiopian

The shoe knows if the stocking has a hole.

Bahamian

A vacant mind is open to all suggestions, as a hollow mountain returns all sounds.

Chinese

The bitterness of studying is preferable to the bitterness of ignorance.

Tagalog (Filipino)

The best candle is understanding.

Welsh

It is better to be ignorant than mistaken.

Japanese

The monkey knows which limb to swing on.

Belizean

Action is the proper fruit of knowledge.

English

Allah preserve us from "Had I only known!"

Hausa (West African)

No one knows so much about the pot as does the spoon.

Andean (Latin American)

LEADERSHIP

Even the largest army is nothing without a good general.

Afghan

Two captains sink a ship.

Turkish

If the townspeople are happy, look for the chief.

Liberian

A gentle hand may lead even an elephant by a hair.

Iranian

The awakening of a giant shakes the world.

Arabic

A great one must have a long heart.

Ethiopian

If you cannot serve, you cannot rule.

Bulgarian

When one chief dies, another arises.

Maori

The higher the monkey climbs, the more it is exposed to danger.

Belizean

The master of the people is their servant.

Yemeni

 LIFE AND LIVING

Life is the source of all things.

Japanese

As the spokes of a wheel are attached to the hub, so all things are attached to life.

Sanskrit

The more shoots, the more leaves.

Malay

Life is like a lamp-flame; it needs a little oil now and then.

Kashmiri

Every day of your life is a page of your history.

Arabic

Life is the greatest bargain—we get it for nothing.

Yiddish

Life is short and full of blisters.

African-American

Whoever has walked with truth generates life.

Sumerian

Live your own life, for you will die your own death.

Latin

The fall of a leaf is a whisper to the living.

Danish

 **LOVE**

A life without love is like a year without summer.

Swedish

Since love departs at dawn, create, O God, a night that has no morn.

Hindi (Asian Indian)

Love is blind—but not the neighbors.

Mexican

Man, woman, and love originated fire.

Spanish

Love never dies of starvation, but often of indigestion.

French

Tell me whom you love, and I'll tell you who you are.

African-American

Cultivate a heart of love that knows no anger.

Cambodian

The one who loves you will make you weep.

Argentine

Love is like fog—there is no mountain on which it does not rest.

Hawaiian

For news of the heart ask the face.

Guinean

 LUCK

The day you decide to do it is your lucky day.

Japanese

Luck is loaned, not owned.

Norwegian

A lucky person is someone who plants pebbles and harvests potatoes.

Greek

In bad luck, hold out; in good luck, hold in.

German

A person is unlucky who falls on his back and breaks his nose.

French

To have luck needs little wit.

Italian

When fortune turns against you, even jelly breaks your teeth.

Iranian

The person afraid of bad luck will never know good.

Russian

There's plenty of time to bemoan bad fortune once it arrives.

Yiddish

A person does not seek luck; luck seeks the person.

Turkish

MARRIAGE

Love is often the fruit of marriage.

French

Before you marry keep both eyes open; after marriage shut one.

Jamaican

Not all who make love make marriages.

Russian

Every pot will find its lid.

Yiddish

A beautiful bride needs no dowry.

Assyrian

When husband and wife live in harmony, they can dry up the ocean without a bucket.

Vietnamese

A person without a spouse is like a vase without flowers.

Cape Verde Islander

To marry once is a duty, twice a folly, and three times—
madness.

Dutch

If you want to marry wisely, marry your equal.

Spanish

One who marries for love alone will have bad days but good
nights.

Egyptian

 **MONEY**

Give me money, not advice.

Portuguese

If you throw money away with your hands, you'll seek it
later with your feet.

Italian

In God we trust—all others pay cash.

American

Money makes even dogs dance.

French

Money buys everything but good sense.

Yiddish

With money, a dragon—without it, a worm.

Chinese

Money is sharper than a sword.

Ashanti (West African)

Money swore an oath that nobody that did not love it should ever have it.

Irish

When money speaks, truth keeps silent.

Russian

Money talks—everything else walks.

African-American

 ## Nature

Though God is almighty, he doesn't send rain from a clear sky.

Afghan

Earth is dearer than gold.

Estonian

A forest that has sheltered you, you should not call a patch of scrub.

Oji (West African)

The day has eyes, the night has ears.

Scottish

The earth produces all things and receives all again.

Spanish

The bird leaves no trail.

Thai

The winter does not leave without a backward glance.

Finnish

Nature is the art of God.

Latin

No matter how fast moonlight runs, daylight catches up.

Virgin Islander

Of all the plants that cover the earth and lie like a fringe of
hair upon the body of our grandmother, try to obtain
knowledge that you may be strengthened in life.

Winnebago (Native American)

 ## OPPORTUNITY

New day—new fate.

Bulgarian

No pear falls into a shut mouth.

Italian

One who waits for chance may wait a year.

Yoruba (West African)

If the eyes didn't see, the hands wouldn't take.

Yiddish

It's a poor mouse that sits on the meal sack and doesn't gnaw.

German

Our faults provide opportunities for others.

Tamil (Asian Indian)

Opportunities come but do not linger.

Nepalese

A tree near the road is easily felled.

Serbian

Where there is sugar, there are ants.

Ilocano (Filipino)

A person who misses a chance and the monkey who misses
its branch can't be saved.

Asian Indian

 PARADOX

Be like a camel—carrying sweets but dining on thorns.

Hindi (Asian Indian)

A silent mouth is musical.

Irish

Too much sugar is bitter.

Nepalese

What was hard to bear is sweet to remember.

Portuguese

The eagle was killed by an arrow made with its own feathers.

Armenian

The smallest pepper is hottest.

Malay

The one who is born yells; the one who dies is silent.

Russian

The one who understands does not speak; the one who speaks does not understand.

Chinese

The art of pleasing is the art of deceiving.

French

A candle lights others and consumes itself.

English

PARENTS AND CHILDREN

Children have more need of models than critics.

French

When you have children, you begin to understand what you owe your parents.

Japanese

Give an extra piece of cake to a stepchild.

Korean

Midsummer night is not long but it sets many cradles rocking.

Swedish

What children say, they have heard at home.

Wolof (West African)

Parents can give their children everything except good fortune.

Yiddish

God could not be everywhere, therefore he made mothers.

Hebrew

The pumpkin vine never bears watermelons.

Belizean

You can do anything with children if only you play
with them.

German

Dearer than our children are the children of our children.

Egyptian

 PATIENCE

The slower you go, the farther you will be.

Russian

Haste has no blessing.

Swahili (East African)

Long is not forever.

German

The salt of patience seasons everything.

Italian

The continuous drip polishes the stone.

Peruvian

At the gate of patience there is no crowding.

Moroccan

Sit and wait for the good chestnuts.

Samoan

Grain by grain, a loaf—stone by stone, a castle.

Yugoslavian

At the bottom of patience one finds heaven.

Kanuri (West African)

The remedy against bad times is to have patience with them.

Arabic

PERMANENCE AND CHANGE

An hour may destroy what an age was building.

English

When the moon is full, it begins to wane.

Japanese

Life is like the moon: now full, now dark.

Polish

As the sun's shadow shifts, so there is no permanence
on earth.

Afghan

A decision made at night may be changed in the morning.

Samoan

The sea becomes the shore, the shore becomes the sea.

Indonesian

The top of the mast now, firewood soon.

Burmese

At high tide fish eat ants; at low tide ants eat fish.

Thai

The winds of heaven change suddenly; so do human fortunes.

Chinese

Time builds castles, and time destroys them.

Serbian

PERSEVERANCE AND PROCRASTINATION

A little ax can cut down a big tree.

Jamaican

Beginning is easy—continuing hard.

Japanese

If not today—when?

Kashmiri

One's utmost moves the heavens.

Korean

Persist as resolutely as you persist in eating.

Maori

A person always breaking off from work never finishes anything.

Nigerian

Mañana is often the busiest day of the week.

Spanish

If you wish to drown, don't torture yourself with shallow water.

Bulgarian

By going and coming, a bird weaves its nest.

Ashanti (West African)

I have so much to do that I am going to bed.

Savoyard (French)

PERVERSITY

One man's beard is on fire, and another warms his hands at it.

Kashmiri

The new boat will find the old stones.

Estonian

The better the fruit, the more wasps to eat it.

German

When the curry is tasty, the rice is hard.

Malay

Happiness is like crystal—when it shines the most, it soon cracks.

Turkish

Useful trees are cut down first.

Korean

The farmer grows the corn, but the bear eats it.

Nepalese

Trouble rains on those already wet.

Spanish

Truth came to market but could not be sold; however, we buy lies with ready cash.

Yoruba (West African)

A year's care, a minute's ruin.

Tagalog (Filipino)

 **PLANNING**

It is not enough to run; you must start in time.

French

Coincidence defeats a well-laid plan.

Tagalog (Filipino)

If you don't have a plan for yourself, you'll be part of someone else's.

American

What good is running if you're on the wrong road?

German

Don't ignore the small things—the kite flies because of its tail.

Hawaiian

Choose your neighbors before you buy your house.

Hausa (West African)

Plan your life at New Year's, your day at dawn.

Japanese

Any plan is bad that cannot be changed.

Italian

Begin with an error of an inch and end by being a thousand miles off the mark.

Chinese

Deliberate slowly, execute promptly.

English

 ## PRACTICALITY

Think of many things—do one.

Portuguese

Keep a thing seven years and you'll find a use for it.

Gaelic

Apple blossoms are beautiful, but rice dumplings are better.

Japanese

Better to ask twice than to lose your way.

Danish

First food, then religion.

Afghan

Any water in the desert will do.

Arabic

Everything is good for something.

Italian

Gather the breadfruit from the farthest branches first.

Samoan

What's the use of consulting a dead person's horoscope?

Singhalese

Don't look where you fell, but where you slipped.

Liberian

PRAYER

Pray as though no work could help, and work as though no prayer could help.

German

Good deeds are the best prayer.

Serbian

Prayer only from the mouth is no prayer.

Jamaican

I never ask God to give me anything; I only ask him to put me where things are.

Mexican

If you want to tell anything to heaven, tell it to the wind.

Oji (West African)

God provides, but he needs a nudge.

Iranian

If you pray for another, you will be helped yourself.

Yiddish

Don't say amen to an unacceptable prayer.

Turkish

Persons ignorant of prayer—let them go to sea.

Italian

A single prayer moves heaven.

Japanese

 PRIDE

Pride is the mask we make of our faults.

Hebrew

An empty sack can't stand up; a full sack cannot bend.

Virgin Islander

A big tree attracts the gale.

Chinese

The blind cannot see—the proud will not.

Russian

The nobler the blood, the less the pride.

Danish

Hunger brings people down, but pride can help them rise.

Mexican

By pride one causes virtue to decline.

Tibetan

The higher you climb, the heavier you fall.

Vietnamese

A fisherman never says his fish stink.

Belizean

Pride extends the length one can spit.

Zairean

 ## PROVERBS

All old sayings have something in them.

Icelandic

Hold fast to the words of your ancestors.

Maori

Proverbs are the daughters of experience.

Sierra Leonean

When the occasion arises, the proverb arrives.

Oji (West African)

Proverbs are little gospels.

Spanish

A proverb is to speech what salt is to food.

Arabic

A proverb is shorter than a bird's beak.

Swiss

As the country, so the proverb.

German

What everyone says must be true.

Hebrew

Proverbs are the people's wisdom.

Russian

 PRUDENCE

If you don't see the bottom, don't wade.

Scottish

If the bird hadn't sung, it wouldn't have been shot.

Japanese

The prudent embark when the sea is calm—the rash when it's stormy.

Maori

Eggs have no business dancing with stones.

Haitian

One must not play on the nose of a sleeping bear.

German

If you can't dance well, you'd better not get up.

Hausa (West African)

Don't sail out farther than you can row back.

Danish

Fools and madmen ought not to be left in their own company.

English

Tread on thorns with your shoes on.

Hebrew

Beware the person with nothing to lose.

Italian

RELATIVE WORTH

In times of need a pig is called uncle.

Albanian

One and one are sometimes eleven.

Kashmiri

Better twice remembered than once forgotten.

German

The stars shine brightest when the moon is gone.

Hausa (West African)

Bad is called good when worse happens.

Norwegian

The best part of repentance is a little sinning.

Arabic

If you had teeth of steel, you could eat iron coconuts.

Singhalese

It's not as good with money as it is bad without it.

Yiddish

A little water is a sea to an ant.

Afghan

It is better to be the head of a chicken than the rear end of an ox.

Japanese

REWARDS AND CONSEQUENCES

One cannot ski so softly that the traces cannot be seen.

Finnish

You can't take milk back from coffee.

Jamaican

We are the authors of our own disasters.

Latin

Where there's a carcass, there will be vultures.

Malay

A tree falls the way it leans.

Walloon

Those not ruled by the rudder will be ruled by the rocks.

Welsh

If you don't scale the mountain, you can't view the plain.

Chinese

No sleep, no dreams.

Korean

The one who doesn't listen will feel.

Swiss

Come for your inheritance and you may have to pay for the funeral.

Yiddish

✒ SELF-RELIANCE

Food tastes best when you eat it with your own spoon.

Danish

Your own rags are better than another's gown.

Hausa (West African)

If you want your eggs hatched, sit on them yourself.

Haitian

Depend on your walking-stick, not on other people.

Japanese

Pray to God, but continue to row toward shore.

Russian

Those who tickle themselves may laugh when they please.

German

A burden that one chooses is not felt.

Italian

Your hand is never the worse for doing its own work.

Welsh

Depend on others and you'll go hungry.

Nepalese

Don't borrow another's nose to breathe with.

Thai

 ## THE SEXES

Men make laws; women make morals.

French

Women are like raindrops—some fall on palaces, others on ricefields.

Vietnamese

A man without a woman is a tree without leaves and branches.

Corsican

Men are as old as they feel, women as old as they look.

Italian

Pride and dignity would belong to women if only men would leave them alone.

Egyptian

Beautiful woman, beautiful trouble.

Jamaican

All women are heirs to Mother Eve.

Yiddish

A woman's first advice is her best.

German

The spouse of a woman is a man, the spouse of a man is his livelihood.

Asian Indian

Vive la différence.

French

STRENGTH AND WEAKNESS

The firm tree does not fear the storm.

Dayak (Indonesian)

Hurrying and worrying are not the same as strength.

Hausa (West African)

If you ford the river in a crowd, the crocodiles won't get you.

Malagasy

A fortress surrenders from within.

Bulgarian

A single arrow is easily broken; a bundle of ten is not.

Japanese

Rocks need no protection from the rain.

Malay

The talkers aren't strong; the strong don't talk.

Burmese

The strong don't need clubs.

Singhalese

Cunning is better than strength.

Bahamian

A day-old pigeon cannot fly over a mountain pass.

Korean

SUCCESS AND FAILURE

From walking—something; from sitting—nothing.

Bulgarian

Self-assurance is two-thirds of success.

Gaelic

The one who wins plays best.

German

All kinds of birds flock to a fruitful tree.

Singhalese

Stupid solutions that succeed are still stupid solutions.

Yiddish

It's not enough to know how to ride—one must also know how to fall.

Mexican

If you like things easy, you'll have difficulties; if you like problems, you'll succeed.

Laotian

We learn little from victory, much from defeat.

Japanese

It is the mind that wins or loses.

Nepalese

Success has many parents, but failure is an orphan.

American

TEMPTATION

The crow may be caged, but its thoughts are in the cornfield.

Belizean

Gold is the devil's fishhook.

Italian

Never pick up what you didn't put down.

Virgin Islander

Shut your door and make your neighbor good.

Portuguese

Because of the bait the crane lost its life.

Vietnamese

The devil catches most souls in a golden net.

German

All temptations are found in either hope or fear.

English

The Great Way is very easy, but all love the bypaths.

Chinese

One should eat sand rather than fall to villainy.

Spanish

The devil tempts but doesn't force.

Guyanan

 Thrift

Scatter with one hand, gather with two.

Welsh

Use it up, make do, or do without.

American

Hobbies cost more than Arabian horses.

German

Save money and money will save you.

Jamaican

Manage with bread and salted butter until God brings something to eat with it.

Moroccan

Spending is quick, earning is slow.

Russian

Economy is the wealth of the poor and the wisdom of the rich.

French

If you buy cheap meat, you'll smell what you have saved when it boils.

Arabic

From saving comes having.

Scottish

If you buy what you don't need, you steal from yourself.

Swedish

TIME AND TIMELINESS

The person who comes last sees least.

Norwegian

Sleep faster—we need the pillows.

Yiddish

Once the rice is pudding, it's too late to reclaim the rice.

Indonesian

If the time is past, preparation does no good.

Yemeni

In bad things be slow; in good things be quick.

Afghan

There is no hand to catch time.

Bengali (Asian Indian)

You can't buy an inch of time with an inch of gold.

Chinese

Today can't catch tomorrow.

Jamaican

Time is the best adviser.

Greek

Time is longer than rope.

Virgin Islander

TRUTH AND FALSEHOOD

Truth may walk through the world unarmed.

Bedouin

Craftiness must have clothes, but truth loves to go naked.

English

Over truth there is light.

Moroccan

Truth is the safest lie.

Yiddish

Liars need good memories.

French

A good lie finds more believers than a bad truth.

German

A lie has no author, nor a liar a conscience.

Hindi (Asian Indian)

The path of a liar is short.

Swahili (East African)

If you lie and then tell the truth, the truth will be considered a lie.

Sumerian

One who lies for you will also lie against you.

Bosnian

✎ VANITY AND ARROGANCE

Every ass loves to hear himself bray.

English

Egotism is an alphabet of one letter.

Scottish

The head of a monkey, the headgear of a prince.

Japanese

Boasting during the day but humble in the dark.

Maori

You arrive Mr. Big Shot but leave Mr. Nobody.

Zulu (South African)

We are both queens—so who will hang the laundry?

Hindi (Asian Indian)

The fly on the water buffalo's back thinks itself taller than the water buffalo.

Tagalog (Filipino)

Vanity blossoms but bears no fruit.

Nepalese

The drum makes a great fuss because it's empty.

Trinidadian

Clouds that thunder do not always rain.

Armenian

 ## VIGILANCE

God gives but does not lock the gate.

Bulgarian

Though near shore, you're still in the ocean.

Malay

Beware of the door with too many keys.

Portuguese

Respect spiritual beings but keep your distance.

Chinese

When a thief kisses you, count your teeth.

Yiddish

Be peaceful yet vigilant—a sheep will bite a person without a stick.

Hindi (Asian Indian)

Beware, the enemy lies under your blanket.

Indonesian

Tap even a stone bridge before crossing it.

Korean

The hardest person to awaken is the person already awake.

Tagalog (Filipino)

Be ever vigilant, but never suspicious.

English

 WAR AND PEACE

War is sweet to those who haven't experienced it.

Latin

Happy nations have no history.

Belgian

The soldiers' blood, the general's name.

Jamaican

In peace be faithful; in war be valiant.

Maori

God grant me a good sword and no use for it.

Polish

May it end with threats and not come to blows.

Samoan

To live in peace one must be blind, deaf, and mute.

Turkish

You can't have peace longer than your neighbor pleases.

Dutch

Bury the hatchet beneath the root of the tree.

Native American

War ends nothing.

Zairean

〜 WEALTH AND POVERTY

Worldly prosperity is like writing on water.

Telugu (Asian Indian)

The poor are the silent of the land.

Mesopotamian

Trusting in riches is like seeking feathers from turtles.

Singhalese

If the rich could hire others to die for them, the poor could make a nice living.

Yiddish

The person who gives is a person who has.

Lithuanian

The devil dances in empty pockets.

Tudor (English)

Wealth is both an enemy and a friend.

Nepalese

Money grows on the tree of persistence.

Japanese

It's no disgrace to be poor, but it can be inconvenient.

Danish

Wealth is but dung, useful only when spread.

Chinese

WISDOM

When you say one thing, the clever person understands
three.

Chinese

One who is unknowingly prophetic has a holy mouth.

Lakota (Native American)

Wisdom is easy to carry but difficult to gather.

Czech

Some are wise and some are otherwise.

English

The wise do as much as they should, not as much as
they can.

French

There is often wisdom under a shabby coat.

Latin

A blind person who sees is better than a seeing person who is blind.

Iranian

The wise understand by themselves; fools follow the reports of others.

Tibetan

The dying cannot leave their wisdom or experience to their heirs.

Italian

One head cannot hold all wisdom.

Maasai (East African)

WORDS AND DEEDS

A tale is soon told; a deed is not soon done.

Russian

Words are mere bubbles of water; deeds are drops of gold.

Tibetan

We make large promises to avoid making small presents.

French

Don't let your tongue say what your head may pay for.

German

Deeds are fruits, words are leaves.

English

Long tongue—short hands.

Czech

A speaker needs no tools.

Nepalese

The sheik's miracles are those of his own telling.

Turkish

The best words give no food.

Gambian

With the mouth one can ford the wildest river.

Ethiopian

 **WORK**

While the sun is still up, let people work that the earth may live.

Hawaiian

To get eggs there must be some cackling.

Dutch

The work will teach you.

Estonian

God gives all birds their food but does not drop it into their nests.

Danish

Mediocrity is climbing molehills without sweating.

Icelandic

Be the first in the field, the last to the couch.

Chinese

It is better to wear out one's shoes than one's sheets.

Genovese (Italian)

You make the road by walking on it.

Nicaraguan

It is easier to give orders than to work.

Lithuanian

When mosquitoes work, they bite and then they sing.

Malian

YOUTH AND AGE

Youth is beauty, even in cattle.

Egyptian

If summer had a mother, she would weep at summer's passing.

Lebanese

The first half of life is spent in longing for the second—the second half in regretting the first.

French

Being young is a fault that diminishes daily.

Swedish

Old canoes can be restored, but not youth and beauty.

Maori

Eat coconuts while you have teeth.

Singhalese

The memories of one's youth make for long, long thoughts.

Lapp

Everyone wants to live long, but no one wants to be called old.

Icelandic

The old one who is loved is winter with flowers.

German

Everyone is the age of their heart.

Guatemalan

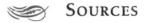 # SOURCES

Abbas, S. R. S. *Kamus Peribahasa*. Bandung, Indonesia: Penerbit Angkasa, 1987.

Akiyama, Aisaburo. *Japanese Proverbs and Proverbial Phrases*. Japan: Japan Welcome Society, 1935.

Anderson, Izelt and Frank Cundall. *Jamaica Negro Proverbs and Sayings*. London: The Institute of Jamaica, 1927.

Auden, W. H. and Louis Kronenberger. *The Viking Book of Aphorisms*. New York: Viking Press, 1962.

Ayalti, Hanan J., ed. *Yiddish Proverbs*. New York: Schocken Books, 1949.

Bayan, R. G., trans. *Armenian Proverbs and Sayings*. Venice: Academy of S. Lazarus, 1909.

Bellesteros, Octavio A. *Mexican Proverbs*. Austin, TX: Eakin Press, 1979.

Benham, W. Gurney. *Putnam's Dictionary of Thoughts*. New York: G. P. Putnam's & Sons, 1930.

Bhamorabutr, Abha. *Thai Proverbs with Their Literal Meanings*. Bangkok, 1980.

Bigelow, John. *The Wit and Wisdom of the Haitians*. New York: Scribner and Armstrong, 1877.

Bohn, Henry G. *A Hand-Book of Proverbs*. London: George Bell & Sons, 1905.

Boehmer, Edward ed. *Churwälsche Sprichwörter.* 1885.

Bosson, James E. *A Treasury of Aphoristic Jewels: The Subhasitaratunanidhi of Saskya Pandita in Tibetan and Mongolian.* Bloomington: Indiana University Press, 1969.

Bronson, Ruth Muskrat. *Indians Are People Too.* New York: Friendship Press, 1944.

Buchanan, Daniel Crump. *Japanese Proverbs and Sayings.* Norman, OK: University of Oklahoma Press, 1965.

Burckhardt, John Lewis. *Arabic Proverbs; or the Manners and Customs of the Modern Egyptians.* London: Bernard Quaritch, Harrison & Sons Printers, 1830.

Burton, Richard F. *Wit and Wisdom from West Africa.* New York: Negro Universities Press, 1865, Biblo and Tannen, 1969.

Carbajo, Antonio, comp. and interp. *Spanish Proverbs.* Miami: Language Research Press, 1964.

Champion, Selwyn Gurney, M.D. *Racial Proverbs: A Selection of the World's Proverbs Arranged Linguistically.* New York: Barnes and Noble, 1938, 1950, 1963.

Christy, Robert. *Proverbs, Maxims and Phrases of All Ages,* vols. 1 and 2. New York and London: G. P. Putnam's Sons, 1889.

Christian, John. *Behar Proverbs.* New Delhi: Unity Book Service, 1891. Reprint, 1986.

Davidoff, Henry. *A World Treasury of Proverbs from Twenty-five Languages.* New York: Random House, 1946.

de Bryne, Josefina Montano. *Proverbios, Adagios, Aforismos, Dichos y Refranes.* Guatemala, 1969.

Delano, Issaac O. *Owe L'es in Oro: Yoruba Proverbs—Their Meaning and Usage,* n.p., n.d.

Elkhadem, Saad, ed. *Egyptian Proverbs and Popular Sayings.* Canada: York Press Ltd, 1987.

Elwell-Sutton, L. P. *Persian Proverbs.* London: John Murray, 1951.

Eugenio, Damiana L. *Philippine Proverb Lore.* Quezon City, Philippines: Philippine Folklore Society, 1975.

Gaffney, Sean and Seamus Cashman, eds. *Proverbs and Sayings of Ireland.* Dublin: Wolfhound Press, 1974.

Galland, Monsieur. *The Remarkable Sayings, Apothegms and Maxims of the Eastern Nations.* London: Richard Baldwin, 1695.

Gordon, Edmund I. *Sumerian Proverbs, Glimpses of Everyday Life in Ancient Mesopotamia.* New York: Greenwood Press, 1968.

Grey, Sir George. *Proverbial and Popular Sayings of the Ancestors of the New Zealand Race (Ko Nga Whakapepeha...).* Cape Town, South Africa: Saul Solomon and Co., 1857.

Guiterman, Arthur. *Betel Nuts: What They Say in Hindustan.* San Francisco and New York: Paul Elder and Co., 1907.

James, Joseph. *The Way of Mysticism.* London: Joseph Cape, 1950.

Jensen, Herman. *A Classified Collection of Tamil Proverbs.* London: Kegan Paul, 1897.

Ha, Tae Hung. *Maxims and Proverbs of Old Korea.* Seoul: Yonsei University Press, 1970.

Haigh, Richmond. *An Ethiopian Saga.* London: George Allen and Unwin, Ltd., 1919.

Hamilton, A. W. *Malay Proverbs: Bidal Melayu.* Singapore: Donald Moore, 1957.

Hart, Henry H. trans. *Seven Hundred Chinese Proverbs.* California: Stanford University Press, 1937.

Hearn, Lafcadio. *Gombo Zhèbes: Little Dictionary of Creole Proverbs.* New York: Will H. Coleman, 1885.

Heckewelder, John. *The First American Frontier: History, Manners, and Customs of the Indian Nations Who Once Inhabited Pennsylvania and the Neighboring States.* New York: Arno Press and *The New York Times,* 1876 (reprint 1971).

Heuries, A. Doris Banks. *Liberian Folklore: A Compilation of Ninety-nine Folktales with Some Proverbs.* London: Macmillan Co., Ltd., 1966.

Hoard, Walter B. *Anthology: Quotations and Sayings of People of Color.* San Francisco: R & E Research Associates, 1973.

Japanese Proverbs and Traditional Phrases. Mt. Vernon, NY: Peter Pauper Press, 1962.

Judd, Henry P. *Hawaiian Proverbs and Riddles.* Honolulu, HA: The Museum, 1930. Reprint, Millwood, NJ: Kraus Reprint Co., 1978.

Karadschisch, W. S. *Volksmärchen der Serben.* Berlin: Georg Reimer, 1854.

Kihau, Eci, collector. *Wisdom of Fiji.* Institute of Pacific Studies of the South Pacific and the South Pacific Social Sciences Association, 1981.

King, Anita. *Quotations in Black.* Westport, CN: Greenwood Press, 1981.

Kirk-Greene, A. H. M. *Huusa Ba Dabo Ba Ne: A Collection of 500 [Hausa] Proverbs.* Ibadan: Oxford University Press, 1966.

Klagsbrun, Francine. *Voices of Wisdom: Jewish Ideals and Ethics for Everyday Living.* New York: Pantheon, 1980.

Knowles, J. Hinton. *A Dictionary of Kashmiri Proverbs and Sayings.* Bombay, India: Education Society's Press, 1885.

Kohere, Reweti T. *He Konae Aroni: Maori Proverbs and Sayings.* Wellington, NZ: A. H. and A. W. Reed, 1951.

Lai, T. C. *Selected Chinese Sayings.* Hong Kong: University of Hong Kong, 1960.

Lall, Kesar. *Nepalese Book of Proverbs.* Kathmandu, Nepal, 1985.

Landsberger, Artur. *Jüdische Sprichwörter.* Leipzig, Germany: Ernst Rowohlt Verlag, 1912.

Leslan, Charlotte and Wolf, comps. *African Proverbs.* Mt. Vernon, NY: Peter Pauper Press, 1962.

Liffring-Zug, Joan, ed. *Scandinavian Proverbs.* Monticello, Iowa: Penfield Press, 1985.

Lindfors, Beruth and Oyekan Owomoyela. *Yoruba Proverbs: Translation and Annotation.* Ohio University, 1973.

Long, J., Rev. *Eastern Proverbs and Emblems*. New York: Funk and Wagnalls, 1895.

Marcus, Russell. *Lao Proverbs*. Bangkok: Craftsman Press, Ltd, 1969.

Marvin, Dwight Edwards. *The Antiquity of Proverbs*. New York and London: G. P. Putnam's Sons, The Knickerbocker Press, 1922.

Marvin, Dwight Edwards. *Curiosities in Proverbs,* vol. 1 and 2. New York: G. P. Putnam's Sons, The Knickerbocker Press, 1916.

Massek, A. ol' Oloisolo and J. O. Sidai. *Edeno O Lmaasai (Wisdom of the Maasai)*. Transafrica Publishers, 1974.

Mauch, Thomas Karl. *The Role of the Proverbs in Early Tudor Literature*. Dissertation. Los Angeles: UCLA, June 1963.

Mawr, E. S. *Proverbele RomaniLor*. London: Kerby and Endeau, 1882.

Merrick, G. *Hausa Proverbs*. New York: Negro Universities Press, Division of Greenwood Publishing Corporation, 1905, 1969.

National Proverbs of France, vol. 5. Philadelphia: David McKay, Publisher, n.d.

National Proverbs: India. London: Cecil Palmer and Hayword, 1916.

National Proverbs of Ireland, vol. 8. Philadelphia: David McKay, Publisher, n.d.

National Proverbs of Italy, vol. 9. Philadelphia: David McKay, Publisher, n.d.

National Proverbs of Spain, vol. 13. Philadelphia: David McKay, Publisher, n.d.

Owens, Patrick and Kulaya Campiranonta. *Thai Proverbs.* Bangkok, Thailand: Darnsutha Press Co., 1988.

Pahk, Induk. *The Wisdom of the Dragon.* New York: Harper & Row, 1970.

Parker, Carolyn Ann. *Aspects of a Theory of Proverbs: Contexts and Messages of Proverbs in Swahili.* Dissertation. Ann Arbor, MI: Xerox University Microfilms, 1974.

Pe, Hla. *Burmese Proverbs.* London: John Murray, 1962.

Peek, Basil. *Bahamian Proverbs.* London: John Culmer Ltd., 1949.

Petersen, Arona. *Herbs and Proverbs of the Virgin Islands.* U.S. Virgin Islands: St. Thomas Graphics, 1974, 1975, 1982, 1987.

Prochnow, Herbert V. and Herbert V. Prochnow, Jr. *The Public Speaker's Treasure Chest: A Compendium of Source Materials to Make Your Speech Sparkle.* New York: Harper & Row, 1942, 1964.

Pullar-Strecker, H. *Proverbs for Pleasure.* New York: Philosophical Library, 1955.

Russian Proverbs. Mount Vernon, NY: Peter Pauper Press, 1960.

Salim, Peter. *Advanced Indonesian-English Dictionary.* Jakarta, Indonesia: C. V. Elmore, 1990.

Schleicher, August. *Litauische Märchen, Sprichwörter, Rätsel und Lieder.* Weimar, Germany: Hermann Böhlau, 1857.

Schultz, E. *Proverbial Expressions of the Samoans.* Translated by Brother Herman. Wellington, N.Z.: The Polynesian Society, 1953.

Sederholm, Dr. *Sendungen der Kurländischen Gesellschaft für Literatur und Kunst,* vol. 2. Mitau: Reyher, 1845.

Senanayaka, Alexander Mendis. *Athetha Wakya Deepanya, or A Collection of Singhalese Proverbs, Maxims, Fables.* Colombo, Sri Lanka: Catholic Press, n.d.

Taylor, Archer. *The Proverb.* Cambridge, Massachusetts: Harvard Univ. Press, 1931.

Te, Huynh Dinh. *Selected Vietnamese Proverbs.* Oakland, CA: Center for International Communication and Development, 1988.

Thompson, John Mark. *The Form and Function of Proverbs in Ancient Israel.* The Netherlands: Mouton and Co. N. V., The Hague, 1974.

Thorburn, S. S. *Bannu'; or Our Afghan Frontier.* London: Trübner & Co., 1876.

Ullrich, Karl-Heinz, ed. *Das Goldene Buch der Zitate.* Munich, Germany: Süd-West Verlags-und Vertriebs-GMBH, 1960.

Westermarck, Edward. *Wit and Wisdom in Morocco.* London: George Routledge & Sons, 1930.

Young, Colville N., collector. *Creole Proverbs of Belize.* Belize City, Belize: 1980, 1986.

Zulu Izaga; That Is Proverbs, or Out-of-the-Way Sayings of the Zulus. Collected, Translated, and Interpreted by a Zulu Missionary. Natal, R.S.A.: John Anderson & Co., 1880.